You Are A Published

Author ...

Now What?

ISBN13: 978-1-934947-04-3

Editor: Danee'ta Shine

Printed in the United States of America

Asta's Mission Statement:

To provide quality publishing and professional services to authors through the effective delivery of customer support and personal development.

Table of Contents

𝒮

You Are A Published

Author ...

Now What?

Message from the Publisher

৶

Congratulations on accomplishing your goal of becoming a published author. The journey of becoming published took a lot of hard work, dedication, and commitment, but you did it and we are proud of you.

Many authors have found their voices with Asta Publications. Advances in print-on-demand technology and distribution have made it a lot easier for readers to access books online and through retail outlets.

Our main goal at Asta Publications is to educate and assist aspiring authors in becoming published. Our model of doing business is to provide an author-centered approach, designed to help authors save money while producing quality books. Our contracts are non-exclusive; therefore, we do not own the rights to your work. If a major publishing company wants to sign you, you are free and clear to negotiate.

Asta Publications' books are distributed by Ingram, which makes your books available to over 25,000 retail outlets. Your book is available on Amazon.com, Borders.com, Barnesandnoble.com, BooksAmillion.com, Alibris.com, and many other retail outlets. Does this mean your book will be on the bookshelves in every store? The answer is no, but your book will be available for purchase wherever books are sold. This is possible because of our return policy. All of our books are re-turnable, making it easier for bookstores to stock our books.

Your partnership with Asta Publications doesn't end once your book has been published. We are here to assist you with keep-ing track of your sales, to offer marketing strategies, and to as-sist with book orders. We are here to help you reap the benefits of being a published author!

Thanks again for choosing Asta Publications. We appreciate You!

Assuanta Howard
CEO/Founder

First Things First

Writing is just the beginning of your journey and not the end.

~ Assuanta Howard

According to the article written in Publisher's Weekly, "A staggering 764,448 titles were produced in 2009 by self-publishers and micro-niche publishers, according to statistics released this morning by R.R. Bowker. The number of 'nontraditional' titles dwarfed that of traditional books whose output slipped to 288,355 last year from 289,729 in 2008. Taken together, total book output rose 87% last year, to over 1 million books."

Everyone has a story to tell, and one way of making sure your history, your message, and your creativity are shared with others is to write a book. Congratulations, you are a published author, but that is just the first step. You are also a publisher, promoter, salesman, and accountant.

You've selected to self-publish and that is a wonderful solution to making sure you maintain control over your product. You have joined the ranks of others before you and now it is time for you to learn more about your new business venture.

First things first, what is publishing...

Publishing is the business of producing and disseminating literature or information for public view.

A commercial publisher distributes books under its own imprint. It purchases manuscripts from authors, and handles the cost of producing those manuscripts: cover and interior designing, typesetting, printing, marketing, distribution, etc. The author is not expected to pay any of these costs. The books are owned by the publisher and remain in the publisher's possession until sold and the author receives a portion of sales in the form of royalties.

Vanity or Subsidized publishing is often called Print-on-demand publishing, which is incorrect. Print-on-demand is a technology used to print books on demand. Vanity or Subsidized publishing provides publishing services to assist authors with getting their books to the market for a fee. Depending on the services needed; the costs range from $250 to $10,000. The services include but are not limited to providing: ISBN, barcode, distribution, marketing, editing, printing, cover design, and more. There are many Vanity or Subsidized publishers that provide print-on-demand technology, which is beneficial to authors that do not have the resources to print a truck load of books and/or store them. Asta Publications provides subsidized publishing along with print-on-demand technology.

A self-publisher is an author who establishes a publishing business and is responsible for paying the cost of designing, printing, distributing, marketing, warehousing, and fulfilling the order.

The cost to self-publish ranges from $3,000 to 10,000. The cost covers includes all phases of self-publishing to include: pre-production (editing, cover design, and interior design), production (printing), and post-production (proofreading, marketing, and distribution) costs.

Self-published books are the property of the author and all sales proceeds belong to the author. With the advancement of digital technology, books can be printed on demand, allowing you the freedom of ordering books as needed.

A bad book is as much of a labour to write as a good one; it comes as sincerely from the author's soul.

~ Aldous Huxley

You Are
An
Authorpreneur

Writing is the only thing that, when I do it, I don't feel I should be doing something else.

~ Gloria Steinem

Starting a company is not difficult, but it takes hard work and dedication. Owning a business affords you the opportunity to deduct some of your expenses, such as the purchasing of a computer, paper, printing expenses, magazine subscriptions, mileage, airplane tickets, hotel fees, conferences, web site design, etc.

One of the first decisions that you will have to make as a business owner is how the company should be structured. This decision will have long-term implications, so consult with an accountant and an attorney to help you select the form of ownership that is right for you.

There are different structures to choose from, including the following: sole proprietorship, partnership, corporation, and limited liability company. For the purposes of this guide we will define the aforementioned structures.

■ ■ ■

Sole Proprietorship

The sole proprietorship is a simple, informal structure that is inexpensive to form. It is usually owned by a single person or a marital community. The owner operates the business, is personally liable for all business debts, and can report profit or loss on personal income tax returns.

Advantages

- You are your own boss
- Less government regulation than other forms
- Simple structure
- Ease of formation
- Business losses lower personal tax

Disadvantages

- Risk losing business with death or disability
- Total personal liability
- Profits taxed as personal income
- Limited financial resources
- Limited management potential can only expand with "after tax dollars"

Partnership

Partnerships are inexpensive to form. They require an agreement between two or more individuals or entities to jointly own and operate a business. Profit, loss, and managerial duties are shared among the partners, and each partner is personally liable for partnership debts.

Partnerships do not pay taxes, but must file an informational return. Individual partners report their share of profits and losses on their personal returns.

Advantages

- Simple organization
- Shared personal resources
- Shared financial resources

- The right to select partners

Disadvantages

- Cost of organization
- Unlimited liability
- Limited decision-making
- Limited life of business
- Sharing of profit

Corporation (Inc. or Ltd.)

This is a complex business structure with more start-up costs than many other forms. A corporation is a legal entity separate from its owners, who own shares of stock in the company. Corporations may be subject to increased licensing fees and governmental regulation more than other structures. Profits are taxed both at the corporate level and again when distributed to shareholders.

Shareholders are not personally liable for corporate obligations unless corporate formalities have not been observed; such formalities provide evidence that the corporation is a separate legal entity from its shareholders.Failure to do so may open the shareholders to liability of the corporation's debts. Corporate formalities include: issuing stock certificates, holding annual meetings, recording minutes at the meetings, and electing directors or ratifying the status of existing directors. Seek a qualified attorney to assist with setting up your corporation.

Advantages

- Shared personal resources
- Shared financial resources

- Perpetual life increased management capability
- Easy transfer of business
- Limited personal liability

Disadvantages

- Possibility of double taxation
- Complex organization
- More costly operations
- More complicated management
- More government

Limited Liability Company (LLC)

The LLC is considered advantageous for small businesses because it combines the limited personal liability feature of a corporation with the tax advantages of a partnership and sole proprietorship. Profits and losses can be passed through the company to its members or the LLC can elect to be taxed like a corporation. LLCs do not have stock and are not required to observe corporate formalities. Owners are called members, and the LLC is managed by these members or by appointed managers.

Advantages

- Protection from personal liability for business decisions or actions of the LLC
- Less Recordkeeping
- Sharing of Profits

Disadvantages

- Limited Life
- Self-Employment Taxes

Commitment leads to action. Action brings your dream closer.

~ Marcia Wieder

The Printing
Process

Progress lies not in enhancing what is, but in advancing toward what will be.

~ Kahlil Gibran

There are basically two main options for printing books: offset and digital. Offset printing offers excellent quality, but can be costly when ordering low quantities (less than 1,000). Offset printers also give you the option of using freight delivery or parcel post. Freight delivery has additional costs such as: delivery inside, the use of the lift gate, etc. where as parcel post is UPS, FedEx or regular mail service. Digital printing offers quality close to offset and allows you to print smaller quantities. However, it is not a cost effective option when printing larger quantities.

For example an offset print run of 10,000 copies of a 228 page book may cost you .65 cents per copy. Whereas the same print run using digital technology may cost you $2.00 per copy.

Advantages of offset printing

- Higher image quality, higher resolution and no streaks/ spots
- Works on a wide range of printing surfaces including paper, wood, cloth, metal, leather, rough paper and plastic
- The unit cost goes down as the quantity goes up
- Quality and cost-effectiveness in high volume jobs
- Many modern offset presses use computer-to-plate (as opposed to the older computer-to-film system) further increasing quality

Advantages of digital printing

- Shorter turnaround
- Lower costs for very small print runs
- Availability of variable data printing (database driven, e.g. mailing lists)

The ABC's
of
Branding

Real integrity is doing the right thing, knowing that nobody's going to know whether you did it or not.

~ **Oprah Winfrey**

Creating a brand is both a simple and challenging task. Brand development orchestrates ideas, images and concepts that your colleagues, media outlets, and target audiences walk away with, when they hear your name and or see one of your book covers. Branding is a science of consistently living up to what you market. How many times have you bought something based on advertising, enticing words, and vivid pictures, just to find out later that it was not what you anticipated?

Branding is a guarantee; it is not hype surrounded by smoke and mirrors. It is the steady fulfillment of a promise to your potential readership.

Personal branding involves the essence of who you are; your personality, your credentials, and your attire. The goal of literary branding is to capture the interior significance of authorship, and building brand awareness, while aligning books (products) to an intended audience.

Branding answers the old question: what makes a person buy one book over another?

You have to expect things of yourself before you can do them.

~ Michael Jordan

Marketing & Promotions 101

"Success is the sum of small efforts, repeated day in and day out."

~ Robert Collier

Publishing is a business. Your book is the product and your customers are readers. To successfully sell your book, it is important to identify who your readers are and determine how you will reach them.

Who will buy your book? Everyone is not your audience. One way of determining your audience is by going to your local book store and observing customers in which your book will be located. Write down their ethnicity, gender and approximate age range. Once you've identified your demographics, you are ready to create a strategy to reach out to them. Try to determine the magazines or newspapers they read or web sites they visit. It is important to determine the appropriate promotional tactics suited to your talents and preferences.

Writing the book is just the start.... and you have a lot of work to do to get it into the hands of your readers.

Think about the following questions for a moment:

• Why should anyone purchase your book?
• Who is going to sell your book? How will anyone know you have written a book?
• Do you think everyone is a potential reader of your book?

Those are just a few questions you will need to answer to help you devise a marketing strategy to succeed. Remember, you will be the number one promoter of your book and who better than you to reach your readers.

Unless you've been on the Oprah Winfrey Show or another greatly publicized media outlet you want to start off your marketing efforts locally. Capitalize on the area where you live and gradually expand your efforts after you've saturated your local market. Local media outlets such as radio, television, and newspapers will be more interested in featuring you.

Publicity is very important in getting readership. Publicity creates a buzz about You and Your book. You can hire a publicist to help you, but you can also do it yourself. All you have to do is a little research on how to design a press or media kit, take a professional photo, write your bio, and read articles or books on marketing and promotions. There is a lot of information right at your finger tips, but you must be willing to do the work. Another good way to promote your book is to host your own online radio show. BlogTalkRadio.com is free to join. If you don't want to host your own, seek out other authors or individuals that are hosting shows and you can get them to interview you.

Your number one goal is to convince potential readers to buy your book. But if they don't know you exist, how can they? It is up to you or your publicist to create awareness.

■■■

Some examples of Marketing:

1. Fake publicity stunt
2. Guest blogging- Guest blog on other blogs largely related, or semi-related to your web sites niche

3. Postcards/Bookmarks - Go into the library and/or book-store, and in the section where your book will be placed, and put your postcards and or bookmarks into every book. Karen Quinones Miller, author and literary agent, suggests at a conference I attended, was to go to one of thosenews-paper bins that are usually outside of establishments and purchase one newspaper. While the box is open, place your postcard and/or bookmark inside of the remaining news-papers
4. Sponsor an event
5. Charity donations - You can donate some of your books, clothing, coats, or proceeds from your book to a charity
6. Enter Contests

As a new author it is important for you to connect with your readers by attending as many events as possible. The connec-tion with your readers is one of the most important factors to remember when attempting to sell a product.

One of the best ways to connect with readers is to create an online presence; this is crucial to your book sales. An integral component of your online presence is to have a web site, but, you will also have to drive people to your site. Your web site should contain content features that will interest people and cause them to purchase your book; blogs and virtual book tours are good ways to attract potential readers.

Before you get started on building your web site, you are go-ing to need a domain name and a host. Ipowerweb.com and GoDaddy.com are just two companies that provide this service; they have templates you can use until you can afford to hire a web designer. There are also sites that provide hosting and tem-plates for free, such as Webs.com.

"You can be professional while also 'keeping it real' with your customers. By interacting with customers in a less formal way, you'll build a strong human connection that helps build brand loyalty."

~ David Hauser, co-founder of Grasshopper

Benefits
of
Social
Networking

It's all about people. It's about networking and being nice to people and not burning any bridges.

~ Mike Davidson

In a nutshell social networking or social media marketing is a cost effective and efficient way to get your readers, media, and colleagues familiar with your history and engaged in your products. Some of the major networking sites are: Facebook, Twitter and MySpace. Blogs are also useful tools to engage readers in your literary work. Then Senator Barack Obama led a momentous presidential campaign, which sparked a political movement. The Obama campaign was ushered in by the social networking industry, thus setting a new standard for how political campaigns should be run. In January 2008, I noticed the number (16) of social sites his campaign was affiliated with. Each site was representative of diverse segments of the United States and many had international appeal. Unbeknownst to his opponents and many in the public, the co-founder of Facebook opted to step down from his post and join Barack Obama's campaign, thus lending his expertise to designing the MyBO.org site which allowed supporters to meet and greet each other, host political house parties, register voters, schedule door-to-door campaign activities, and most of all generate the largest amount of political contributions to date. According to the Federal Elections Commission now President Barack Obama raised over 744 million dollars.

In addition, Microsoft also recognized the power of the social network and bought 1.6% of Facebook's stock for $240 million dollars in October 2007. What does this tell authorpreneurs? Use your time and energy to get your brand on the social network highway. It gives you a cost effective method to make connections with your audience, or at least media outlets, that can expand your brand, image and readership. Create an account with Myspace, Facebook, Word-Press, Author Den, and Book Tour accounts. Connect with Asta Publications and Asta PR Services on Facebook and Twitter.

There are several authors promoting their books and listing their events. Contact those locations and schedule a book signing or participate in those events. Attending trade shows and book festivals are great ways to find readers, or potential buyers. Use all of your contacts to network, find creative ways to network and promote your book.

The wonders of social networking and social media marketing allow you the freedom to create accounts for both you as the author and individual sites for each book.

Basic
Media Kit

All books are divisible into two classes, the books of the hour, and the books of all time.

~ John Ruskin

Packaging your message and your expertise is an essential piece to connecting with the media. A media kit, also referred to as a "Press Kit" accentuates your brand. It answers the who, what, when, where, why, and how for interested editors, writers and reporters about your product and or business.

Media kits can be in both digital and print ready formats. If you decide to launch a web site, create a direct press or media kit link. You want to make it easier for the media to learn about you at a glance.

The media kit should include:

- Folder – Be creative with color and texture, but notwith quality. Make sure it has at least one pocket.
- Business Card – Include a business card to serve as a quick contact reference.
- Contact/ Fact Sheet – Include your contact information and where your book can be found.
- Collateral Material – brochures, postcards, flyers with logo or image of your book, and bookmarks
- Author Biography – Compose one to two paragraphs about yourself to highlight and or supplement awards, recognition, expertise, and credentials.
- Head Shot – Make sure it is professional and it is at least 300 dpi (dots per inch) for digital reproduction and 72 dpi for web usage.

- Review Sheet – List the most compelling and substantive reviews that complement your writing and expertise. Use reviews from Amazon andBarnes and Noble
- Articles- include articles written about you. You may in clude articles written online as well.
- Press Releases – Past news features of both you, the author and your material; press releases are a brief synopsis of literary and substantive events that would appeal to media outlets
- Social Media Releases (SMR) – New complimentary public relations tool for the traditional press release; SMR's system engages readers with multi-media content throughout social networking sites and tracking sites, such as Google News, Twitter and Facebook

Getting Your Book Into Bookstores

&

Scheduling Booksignings

We all have dreams. But in order to make dreams come into reality, it takes an awful lot of determination, dedication, self-discipline, and effort.

~ Jesse Owens

Y ou've received your complimentary copies and now you are ready to start selling your books. Your books are available for purchase wherever books are sold, but how do you get them onto the bookshelves? Building relationships and networking is key to any business, particularly the book business. In addition to the major bookstore retailers, there are several local and independently owned stores willing to give you the opportunity to place your books into their stores on a consignment basis.

What is consignment? Consignment is when a bookstore takes a certain number of books to sell. They do not purchase books from you, but will pay you once your books are sold. Each store has its own criteria for acceptance; therefore it is up to you to find out the process for each store.

We suggest that you research a few bookstores in your area and find out what types of books they sell and see if their niche matches with your target audience. Once you've narrowed down your list, find out who orders books for the store and contact him/her. Some small and independently owned bookstores prefer to order books from distributors. If that is the case, let them know your book is distributed by Ingram. If they prefer to put you on consignment, find out how you can get your book into their store and what their consignment rates are. Don't be alarmed if they ask you to send a media kit along with one or two copies of your book. Be sure to find out a good time to follow-up with them regarding acceptance of your book.

Scheduling booksignings, readings, and public appearances are an integral part of your marketing campaign. A booksigning is an event that features you and your book. This is a great opportunity for you to meet potential readers in person. Many readers tend to feel more motivated to purchase a copy of your book if they can connect with you. Readers like to communicate with authors about their books and the opportunity to get a copy signed by the author doesn't hurt at all.

Independent bookstores and larger chain retailers both organize book signings. Your chances for finalizing an appearance are greater with the independents; they are more willing to support local authors. In order to pinpoint potential bookstores, you can conduct an Internet search for local bookstores in your area.

Contact the store and let them know you are interested in doing a book signing at their location. The person answering the phone will direct you to the right person. Remember, these are busy people. Have your press release and pitch sheet ready. Some managers will ask you to submit a media kit and a copy of your book before they will allow you to sign in their store. The manager or community relations manager will want to make sure they can order your books and will ask for your ISBN. Inform them that your books are distributed through Ingram and provide them with the title and ISBN. Don't be alarmed if the book store declines to have you sign at their location; it is their choice to be selective. Move on to the next store on your list. Plan early, because in many cases both the large and small bookstores have their events planned weeks or even months in advance.

Follow-up with prospective bookstores who have not confirmed dates. Be persistent without being annoying. After three or four unsuccessful attempts with a particular store or person, move on to another prospect.

"You've got to be success minded. You've got to feel that things are coming your way when you're out selling; otherwise, you won't be able to sell anything."

~ Benjamin Jowett

Tips

For

Successful

Booksignings

"If a product isn't selling, I want to get it out of there because it's taking up space that can be devoted to another part of my line that moves. Besides, having a product languish on the shelves doesn't do much for our image."

~ Norman Melnick

Once your book is published, get busy, do a booksigning. It can be at a local book store, beauty salon, coffee shop, home, book club, etc. Always be on the look out for opportunities to promote your book. A booksigning is a time to introduce you and your book content to the reading public, for you to share who you are, and to sell readers on why they should invest in your book.

The key to a successful book signing event is to stay abreast of what others are doing. Analyze every book signing event you attend and adapt what you think will work for you. Remain open to new ideas and ways of presenting yourself, and never stop promoting.

Attend author's book signings and observe how they interact with the public. Introduce yourself as an author and check out their table set-up and promotional items. Find out how they found out about the signing. Be friendly and take a look at their book, and if interested, buy it.

With your newly collected information, make a checklist to include a plan of action for the book signing. Create and practice your elevator speech. Have either extra flyers, business cards, postcards, bookmarks, something on hand that you can pass out to help promote the event prior to and on the day of. Make sure you have the correct address and location; print out your MapQuest directions or have your GPS set. Also have your contact's name and telephone number in case you get lost. Most importantly, make sure you have enough books for the signing.

Have a bottle of water and mints. Bookstore staff members tend to be great hosts and will offer to give you a bottle of water or a cup of coffee, but in case they don't, you will be prepared. Do not expect them or ask them to provide you with beverages or food.

Always show up at least 15-20 minutes before your scheduled signing time. This will give you an opportunity to pass out postcards and talk to potential readers about your book. Don't stand around. Take your book, walk around and talk to anyone that will listen. Or you can hand them your information and invite them to stick around for your signing or drop by your table.

Giveaways are always nice. They may not buy your book the day of your booksigning, so you want them to walk away with something that provides them with information about your book, in case they want to purchase your book at another time. Another good idea is to invite them to sign-up for your news-letter or blog.

Having someone to assist you can help the experience go smoother. If you prefer to work alone, prepare to do it all; from introducing yourself, to receiving monies, to signing books and crowd control.

A few pointers to remember:

- Confirm the signing with the manager at least one week in advance.
- Make sure they have you scheduled and your books have arrived, if they had to order them in advance.
- Promote on your end. Tell your friends and family.
- Bring your family and friends to the event. The more, the merrier.
- Make an announcement on any list serves you belong to, like Myspace, Facebook, etc. The more effort you put in, the greater chances of increased attendance. Don't expect the book store to promote you; that's your responsibility.
- Dress comfortably, but nicely for the signing.
- Bring Your Own Water!
- Presentation is everything. Make sure you bring a table-cloth, book holders, poster board, and something that stands out on your table.
- Stand up and be enthusiastic about selling.
- Talk, talk, talk. Don't be afraid to smile, wave, and greet customers.
- Make eye contact. Do not sit there and read a newspaper or magazine, talk on your cell phone… you are there to sell your book.
- Remember, signings are for sales, publicity, and networking. You may or may not sell a lot of books, so the contacts you make are important. You might meet someone who can suggest another venue for you to promote and sell your books.

"Originality is not seen in single words or even sentences. Originality is the sum total of a man's thinking or his writing."

~ Isaac Bashevis

Ordering Books

"The difference between the possible and the impossible lies in a person's determination."

~ Tommy Lasorda

One of the benefits of publishing through Asta Publications is that you can order as little as one book to over ten thousand copies. That's the advantage of print-on-demand. Our packages included complimentary books and you are not obligated to order more. If you opt to order additional copies, you can order them as needed. Asta offers discounts on orders of 500 and above; these discounts range from 5%-25%. Asta also provides discounts on packages and print runs periodically, so make sure you are on our e-mail list to receive the most recent updates.

Online Purchases

Asta titles are available for purchase online at Alibris, Amazon.com, Barnesand Noble.com, BooksAmillion, Borders and several smaller online retailers. Most of our books are printed and shipped within twenty-four hours upon receipt of an order.

Ordering at Local Bookstores

Your book is available for purchase at your local bookstore. There are more books than there is shelf space to stock them, so more than likely your book will have to be special ordered.

Independent and Small Bookstores

Most independent and small bookstores prefer to have a consignment arrangement with you. This means they will take a few copies of your book and pay you a percentage for all books sold.

Ordering your Book from Asta

To purchase copies of your book, please contact Asta Publications' Customer Service Department at 678-814-1320.

Upon receipt of your order, you will receive an e-mail confirmation or phone call. Once your order is ready to be shipped, you will receive an e-mail from us with your UPS tracking number. Book orders cannot be cancelled nor refunded, except in the event of poor quality. Please contact your associate to report quality or quantity issues within three business days of receiving your orders.

Distribution Fees,

Sales Reports,

and

Compensation

"By perseverance the snail reached the ark."

~ Charles H. Spurgeon

Distribution is a critical piece of the publishing puzzle. Most book stores have direct computer access to the Ingram catalog, where they can find any book distributed by Ingram. There is a benefit for bookstores to order from a single source. Asta Publications' distribution is provided by Ingram to over 25,000 retail outlets. (Please note: it takes approximately four weeks for your book to be fully integrated into Ingram's database initially. Please wait until your book is fully available before scheduling book signings.

When you initially signed up for services, distribution was included in your package price. In order to maintain distribution for your book, there is an annual fee. We will send you a reminder notice the month prior to your anniversary date to let you know when payment is due. If you would like to continue having your books available for purchase, the annual renewal fee is $250. If we do not receive payment by the due date, your title will no longer be available for purchase through our distribution channels. If we receive notification after the deadline period and your title is inactive, there will be an additional charge of $100 to reactivate, in addition to the $250.

Sales Reports and Compensation

You will receive a sales report along with payment (when applicable*) on a quarterly basis.

Note the schedule below:

First Quarter	April 30th
Second Quarter	July 31st
Third Quarter	October 31st
Fourth Quarter	January 31st

Compensation is determined by actual sales made through our distribution channels. You will receive payment for books sold minus the cost of printing and the discounts provided to the retailer. To better understand the calculation methods used, note below:

For example:

Your 180 page book retails at $15.00. We provide a discount of 45% to retailers. Retailers are paying $8.25 per book. The cost of printing is $5.50 per book.

During the first quarter your sales report indicates you've sold 5 books from January 1-March 30. Retailers paid $41.25 total for your books. Your total printing costs is $27.50.

Subtract the cost of printing from the retailer's discounted price, and your compensation is $13.75. Your balance of $13.75 will be transferred over to the next quarter. **Checks are issued in amounts of $40 and over.**

Author purchases are not included in this calculation. All monetary transactions are in U. S. dollars only. There is a one-month grace period from sale to the creation of a payment. For example, January through March is the first quarter. We will send your sales report and payment by April 30th. It takes a few weeks for your purchases to appear on your sales report, so don't be concerned if your current sales report doesn't show all of the purchases you believed took place during a given quarter. Because of the number of authors we work with, please do not call us prior to the date your sales report is due to inquire about sales.

*Checks are only issued if the amount owed is forty dollars ($40) and up.

"Know how to ask questions. Most people at trade shows push their products on people. But when you sit back and ask questions, you learn a great deal about the customer."

~ Ted Sun

Frequently
Asked
Questions

"The price of success is hard work, dedication to the job at hand, and the determination that whether we win or lose, we have applied the best of ourselves to the task at hand."

~ Vince Lombardi

1. **What if I did not register my manuscript with the copy-right office prior to publishing my book, is it too late to do it now?**

No, you can send your published version of the book to the Copyright Office.

2. **Can my book be updated after the book has been published?**

Yes, however there is an additional fee to have your book updated.

3. **Can I have my book in a hard cover format as well?**

Yes, for an additional fee, Asta offers the option of making hard cover versions of your book available after your paperback book achieves print-ready status.

4. **Do you offer e-book formats?**

Yes, but there is an additional fee. Contact the main office for more information.

5. **What if I want to make changes to my book after it is complete and available for sale?**

The magnificent thing about print-on-demand is that you can make revisions at anytime. Contact your Publishing Associate for additional information. Note that applicable fees may apply.

6. Where will my book be available for purchase?

Your book will be available for sale through a number of on-line retail and wholesale channels, including Amazon and Barnes & Noble, to name a few. Books are also listed in Books in Print and on Asta's web site.

7. Can bookstores purchase copies of my book and make it available for sale in their store?

Yes, your book will be made available through Baker & Taylor and Ingram. In order to remain competitive and to give your book the edge it needs, all of our books are returnable. It is the publishing industry's standard way of doing business to allow book stores to return books. Book stores will be more amenable to carry your title if they know they can return it.

8. Are discounts offered to bookstores or other vendors?

Bookstores normally receive a 55% discount. Asta Publications offers a 45% discount to book retailers.

9. When can I expect to see my book listed as available for sale?

Once your book is approved by you and is ready for print, your book will become available almost immediately. Allow a minimum of four weeks.

10. Can you provide me with the name and contact information of customers who have bought my book?

No, we are unable to disclose personal information of retail customers who purchase your book, for privacy reasons.

11. What are royalties?

A royalty is the amount of money an author receives for each copy of his or her title that is fulfilled by a publisher.

12. Do you pay royalties and how does that work?

No, Asta does not pay royalties. As the author, you pay for the cost of printing andminus the 45% discounted retailer purchasing prce, and you receive the balance.

13. How are royalties paid?

Asta does not pay royalties. For sales that come through our distributor, you receive the balance from the discounted price given to retail outlets minus the cost of printing. See Publishing Agreement for further information.

14. Does Asta Publications market my book? Or do you have services to assist me in marketing?

As a self-published author, you are responsible for the marketing and promotion of your book. However, we do assist with marketing and promotions on a limited basis.

15. Can you help me schedule booksignings?

Yes, we can assist you with scheduling book signings.

16. How do I order copies of my book?

Ordering copies of your book is simple. Contact the main office and one of our Publishing Associates will assist you.

17. Do I receive a discount when ordering copies of my own book?

Asta has already built-in a discount. If you would like to order 500 or more books, Asta can give you a larger discount.

18. What type of printing does Asta Publications do?

We use state-of-the-art print-on-demand (POD) technology. We also provide off-set printing for larger quantities requested.

19. What is print-on-demand? What are the advantages of this technology?

Print-on-Demand (POD) is a revolution in publishing. POD is a digital process that became commercially viable in the mid-1990's. Using this technology, printers can produce as little as one copy at a time. POD empowers authors to generate customer demand before printing the book. The advantage of POD is that you can print 1 to 10,000 copies of your book.

Resources

Suggested

Reading

"My great concern is not whether you have failed, but whether you are content with your failure."

~ Abraham Lincoln

1. *The Self-Publishing Manual: How to Write, Print and Sell Your Own Book* by Dan Poynter

2. *The Complete Guide to Self-Publishing: Everything you need to know, to write, publish, promote, and sell your own book* by Tom & Marilyn Ross

3. *How to Succeed in the Publishing Game* by Vickie M. Stringer and Mia McPherson

4. *How to Self-Publish for Profit* by Jawar

5. *Get Published* by Susan Driscoll and Diane Gedymin

6. *Publishing for Profit Successful Bottom-Line Management for Book Publishers* by Thomas Woll

7. *The Self-Publishing Journal* by Assuanta Fay Howard

8. *The Copyright Permission and Libel Handbook A Step-By Step Guide for Writers, Editors, and Publishers* by Jassin J. Lloyd and Steven Schechter

9. *Classroom in a Book: Adobe InDesign CS5* by Adobe Systems

10. *Bookmaking* by Marshall Lee

11. *The Chicago Manual of Style* (Latest Edition)

12. *Elements of Style* by William Strunk Jr., E. B. White, and Roger Angell

13. *The McGraw-Hill Handbook of English Grammar and Usage* by Mark Lester and Larry Beason

14. *The McGraw-Hill Desk Reference for Editors, Writers, and Proofreaders* by K.D. Sullivan and Merilee Eggleston

15. *Merriam Webster Dictionary and Thesaurus* Newest Edition

16. *1001 Ways to Market Your Books for Authors and Publishers* by John Kremer

17. *The 22 Immutable Laws of Branding* by Al Ries and Laura Ries

About Asta Publications

Asta Publications, LLC was founded, in 2004 and provides self-publishing services, and brand management and marketing campaigns for literary professionals.

Asta Publications holds membership affiliations with the the following:

- Fulton County Workforce Investment Board
- National Independent Artist Networking Alliance Foundation (NIANAF)
- American Counseling Association
- TheAmerican Society for Training and Development
- Independent Book Publishers Association
- Public Relations Society of America
- The New York Center for Independent Publishing
- The Small Publishers Association of North America
- The Writer's Well

Contact Information:

Main Office: 678-814-1320
Fax Number: 678-814-1350
E-mail: info@astapublications.com

www.astapublications.com

ASTA
PUBLICATIONS ™